Family

brothers

sisters

mother and baby

father and baby

daughter and son

daughter and son

husband and wife

grandfather and grandmother

How many children?

She has 5 children.

How many children?

He has 5 children.

How many children?

He has 2 children.

How many children?

She has 2 children.

How many children?

They have 2 children.

How many children?

They have 6 children.

How many children?

They have 3 children.

How many children?

They have 2 children.

How many children?

She has 5 girls.

How many children?

He has 5 girls.

How many children?

He has 1 girl and 1 boy.

How many children?

She has 1 girl and 1 boy.

How many children?

They have 1 girl and 1 boy.

How many children?

They have 5 boys and 1 girl.

How many children?

They have 1 girl and 2 boys.

How many children?

They have 1 girl and 1 boy.

Easy English Readers:
Family

www.teachabcenglish.com

2016

Made in the USA
San Bernardino, CA
27 April 2018